Little Riddlers

Essex Poets

Edited By Jess Giaffreda

First published in Great Britain in 2018 by:

Young Writers
Remus House
Coltsfoot Drive
Peterborough
PE2 9BF
Telephone: 01733 890066
Website: www.youngwriters.co.uk

All Rights Reserved
Book Design by Ashley Janson
© Copyright Contributors 2018
SB ISBN 978-1-78896-431-9
Printed and bound in the UK by BookPrintingUK
Website: www.bookprintinguk.com
YB0359M

FOREWORD

Dear Reader,

Are you ready to get your thinking caps on to puzzle your way through this wonderful collection?

Young Writers' Little Riddlers competition set out to encourage young writers to create their own riddles. Their answers could be whatever or whoever their imaginations desired; from people to places, animals to objects, food to seasons. Riddles are a great way to further the children's use of poetic expression, including onomatopoeia and similes, as well as encourage them to 'think outside the box' by providing clues without giving the answer away immediately.

All of us here at Young Writers believe in the importance of inspiring young children to produce creative writing, including poetry, and we feel that seeing their own riddles in print will keep that creative spirit burning brightly and proudly.

We hope you enjoy riddling your way through this book as much as we enjoyed reading all the entries.

CONTENTS

Belmont Castle Academy, Grays

Nylah John (7) & Nevayah John	1
Monika Swatek (7)	2
Thomas Ryan (7)	3
Nazim Uddin (7)	4
Ayomide Yusuf (6)	5
Titilayo Bada (6)	6
Olivia Alexander (7)	7
Maehan Suthakaran (7)	8
Berrie Rose Hoyle (7)	9
Alisha Tamang (5)	10
Loui Crooks (7)	11
Rhys Allen (7)	12
Temi Akin-Lawal (7)	13
Cosimo Todor (6)	14
Esme Walker (5)	15
Aleksandra Protasova (7)	16
Maya Brake (5)	17
Liza Jankina (5)	18
Joseph Nifton Mulroue (6)	19

Cranbrook Primary School, Ilford

Sofia Hoque (7)	20
Luke Lyons-Adamson (6)	21
Jan Denderski (7)	22
Uzayr Hussain (7)	23
Alexandra Miron (6)	24
Hadiya Izzat (6)	25
Aleeza Z Qadir (6)	26
Milan Mistry (7)	27
Ayman Patel (7)	28
Sulaiman Patel (7)	29
Shahmeer Khan (7)	30
Mya Kaur (6)	31

Ahmed Ali Ibrahim (7)	32
Anaiyah Shafiq-Robinson (7)	33

Darlinghurst Academy, Leigh-On-Sea

Michael Austin Culloty (6)	34
Elsie Newson (6)	35
Henry Dylan Giles (5)	36
Jeffrey Tinnams (5)	37
Evie Grace Coubrough (5)	38
Freya Cardew (6)	39
Nathaniel Seabrook (5)	40
Nancy Inmonger (6)	41
Miriam Adesida (5)	42
Marilyn Roberts (6)	43
Devon Riley Carrier (6)	44
Mia Forbes (5)	45
Callum Knight (5)	46
Alistair Jopling (5)	47
Florence (6)	48

Five Elms Primary School, Dagenham

Muhammad Azan (6)	49
Jessica Boyd (6)	50
Alara Tufansoy (5)	51
Sean Ampansah (6)	52
Francesca Michaels-Hayter (5)	53
Osayantin Osunbor (6)	54
Jeremy Yeboah (6)	55
Shanujah Jegatheesan (7)	56
Samanta Saldukaite (6)	57
Lily-Belle Bryan (6)	58
Esther Kyerewaa Tabi (5)	59

Lily-May Oyewumi (5)	60
Mariam Musharaf (5)	61
Paul Parkinson (7)	62
Aqeeb Ali (6)	63
Macie Twiggs (6)	64
Moyin Emmanuella Akintunde (7)	65
Annabel Chiamaka Omereonye (6)	66
Alessia Maria Ciorba (6)	67
Bailey Brodie (6)	68
Alfie Martin (5)	69

Furze Infant School, Chadwell Heath

Shakirah Haque (6)	70
James Hernon (6)	71
Hamas Kakar (7)	72
Ademide Elizabeth Ogunmokun (6)	73
Sulaiman Qadir (7)	74
Michaela Atulomah (7)	75
Jakub Powaga (7)	76
Eshaal Fatima Zaidi (6)	77
Ishaq Amin (6)	78
Isabel Ruby Arunachalam (7)	79
Tameem Wahhaj (6)	80
Maeasha Noor (6)	81
Saad Amin Mitru (7)	82
Akashdeep Rylee Singh (6)	83
Jonathan Pinard (6)	84
Raiha Pabani (6)	85
Amina Begum (7)	86
Ali Adeel (7)	87
Issa Renato Morgante (6)	88
Alan Idriss Abiji (6)	89
Leke Toluwanimi Aiyemo-Abiwo (7)	90
Amy Yaa Abiji (6)	91
Anthony Deaconeasa (6)	92
Schalk Steyn (7)	93
Joshua Samuels (7)	94
Monique Isaac (6)	95
Sara Hussain (6)	96
Lale Kussan (6)	97
Milan Vyas (7)	98
Tanjimul Haque (6)	99
Nyah White-Laud (7)	100
Tanisha Qyra Noim (7)	101
Khadijah Jannath (6)	102
Domas Dackevicius (6)	103
Tyler Zachary Frederick (6)	104
Robert Iuzcov (6)	105
Aroush Ashraf Ahasan (6)	106
Zaina Mahmood (7)	107
Eva Mana (7)	108
Tanzeela Hussain (6)	109
Erin Young (6)	110
Aiden Chipungu (6)	111
Jasmine Begum (6)	112
Jayden Richards (7)	113

Gidea Park Primary School, Gidea Park

Joshua Spry (5)	114
Oliver Ian Swider (5)	115
Violet Bulmer (5)	116
Inaya Ahmed (5)	117
Olivia Killick (6)	118
Portia Holton (6)	119
Lexi Zhao (5)	120
Nicole Racila (5)	121
Niharika Sharma (6)	122
Lennaea McGowan (6)	123
Ria Patel (6)	124
Alice Evelyn Corkin (5)	125
George Moore (5)	126
Eirene Kalliopi Palamaras (5)	127
Lola Prescott (6)	128
Henry Wakeling (6)	129
Francesca Davie (6)	130
Alexander Aye (6)	131
Millie Grimes (6)	132
Harrison Sutton-Evans (5)	133
Zachary Tran (5)	134
Chloe Marcou (6)	135

Tia Blenman (6)	136
Jessica Mawer (6)	137
Samuel David Weatherly (6)	138
Kendra Akua Lord (6)	139
Ethan George Bird (6)	140
Kiyarah Thomas (5)	141
Lucie Hawkins (5)	142
Melanie Deleu (6)	143
Rosie Winser-Shead (5)	144
Evan Rejek (5)	145
Tayte Ashcroft (5)	146
Vanaya Joshi (5)	147
Kaiden Chambers (5)	148
Tausif Ornob Islam (5)	149
Fraser Sowerby (6)	150
Toby Morton Woodman (6)	151
Hamish Jhurry (6)	152
William Walker (5)	153
Teja Zeimantaite (6)	154
Jack Sullivan (5)	155
Connor Craydon (6)	156
Dhruv Mistry (6)	157
Jay Cheung (5)	158
Thuy-Trang Nguyen (5)	159
Hafi Kalota (6)	160
Rosie June Taylor (6)	161
Shantel Agyei (5)	162
Marley Henry (5)	163
Mya Blenman (6)	164
Riley Collins (5)	165
Lois Lynch (6)	166
Lukas Lapuska (5)	167

THE POEMS

The Spoiler

I am very loveable.
I'm the best cleaning machine.
I'm the best alarm clock.
I'm a tea drinker.
I am the carrier.
I give the best cuddles.
I make you feel better.
I wipe away your tears when you're sad.
I am always there for you.
Who am I?

Answer: Nylah and Nevayah's mum.

Nylah John (7) & Nevayah John
Belmont Castle Academy, Grays

Slither, Slither

I write an S on the bumpy rumpling floor
I'm as slimy as a slithery gloopy snail.
I come from a tiny egg.
I can be big, medium or small.
I can bite you with my poisonous fangs.
I have no hands, I have no feet.
What am I?

Answer: A snake.

Monika Swatek (7)
Belmont Castle Academy, Grays

The Bluish Creature

I blow water out of my back.
I have a mouth as big as a shark.
I have razor-sharp teeth.
I glide in water.
I have a tail as big as a dragon.
I am a huge sea monster.
I am a slow sea creature.
I am blue.
What am I?

Answer: A whale.

Thomas Ryan (7)
Belmont Castle Academy, Grays

The Rock Flyer

I have a tongue that burns like the sun.
I am long as a metal cruise ship.
My spikes are as long as a knife.
I am hard as a rolling stone.
My hands are as long as a prickly branch.
My legs are as thin as a pipe.
What am I?

Answer: A dragon.

Nazim Uddin (7)
Belmont Castle Academy, Grays

The Sunny Place

I am very playful.
I can be big or small.
I stay in the same place but sometimes move.
Children love to visit me.
I have steep, slippery slopes and sky-high ropes.
Part of me can swing up into the trees.
What am I?

Answer: A playground.

Ayomide Yusuf (6)
Belmont Castle Academy, Grays

Little Jumper

I can hop.
I am little and my ears are tall.
I am white.
My feet are small.
You might see me at the farm.
I am smaller than a cat.
I am faster than a snail.
I have a fluffy tail.
What am I?

Answer: A rabbit.

Titilayo Bada (6)
Belmont Castle Academy, Grays

The Hopping Genius

I am as green as a tree.
I am slimy but look scaly.
I can jump high.
I like swimming in the cool garden pool or pond.
When I make a noise my neck expands.
I leap on circular lily pads.
What am I?

Answer: A frog.

Olivia Alexander (7)
Belmont Castle Academy, Grays

The Meat-Eater

I am a meat-eater.
I have big black stripes which tell me who I am.
I'm very good at hunting.
I run fast.
I am very good at hiding.
I roar very loud.
I have sharp claws.
What am I?

Answer: A tiger.

Maehan Suthakaran (7)
Belmont Castle Academy, Grays

The Cuddliest Animal Ever!

I live in Australia.
I have a black, leathery nose.
I have soft fluffy ears.
I am quite big.
I am a herbivore.
I love to hug eucalyptus trees.
Most of the time.
What am I?

Answer: A koala.

Berrie Rose Hoyle (7)
Belmont Castle Academy, Grays

What Am I?

I am scary like a lion.
I have fire and I have wings.
My skin is colourful and so are my eyes.
My nose is red and so are my hands.
I have a head and it is colourful.
What am I?

Answer: A dragon.

Alisha Tamang (5)
Belmont Castle Academy, Grays

The Leaper

I have massive long ears.
I have big, long feet.
I'm as big as a bed.
I'm really kind.
I carry a baby in my belly.
I'm a giant jumper.
What am I?

Answer: A kangaroo.

Loui Crooks (7)
Belmont Castle Academy, Grays

Mouth-Watering

I am small and squishy.
There are lots of me.
I am yellow.
Before I am thrown into steamy water, I am crunchy and hard.
I like to be put with a tasty sauce.
What am I?

Answer: Pasta.

Rhys Allen (7)
Belmont Castle Academy, Grays

The Water Squirter

I have gigantic floppy ears.
I have soft wrinkly skin.
I love to gobble lots of peanuts.
I am very humongous.
I have a long trunk.
What am I?

Answer: An elephant.

Temi Akin-Lawal (7)
Belmont Castle Academy, Grays

Rrrr!

I am big and I blow scorching fire.
I am not scared of anything.
I have humongous wings.
I am normally red or green.
I can fly.
What am I?

Answer: A dragon.

Cosimo Todor (6)
Belmont Castle Academy, Grays

Colour Changer

I have a tongue longer than a snake.
I eat bugs, like a bat.
I have big eyes for searching for food.
I can change my colour.
What am I?

Answer: A chameleon.

Esme Walker (5)
Belmont Castle Academy, Grays

A Runner

I am as fluffy as a bear.
I am as cheeky as a monkey.
I like to bite.
I have a funny face.
I like to store food.
What am I?

Answer: A hamster.

Aleksandra Protasova (7)
Belmont Castle Academy, Grays

Blossom

I am bigger than a house.
I am green and brown.
I am alive.
I can't move.
I like water.
What am I?

Answer: A tree.

Maya Brake (5)
Belmont Castle Academy, Grays

What Am I?

I am black like a bin.
I have four legs.
I have a black nose.
I have white patterns.
What am I?

Answer: A zebra.

Liza Jankina (5)
Belmont Castle Academy, Grays

What Am I?

I am as big as a house.
My wings are as long as a graph.
I am as red as the boiling sun.
What am I?

Answer: A dragon.

Joseph Nifton Mulroue (6)
Belmont Castle Academy, Grays

Red Town

I am red and I leap.
I make more of me when I go near wood.
I make people scream away from me.
I harm and kill people.
I don't know why.
I just blaze human beings to death.
I spread quickly all over houses and shops.
They can't get rid of me until they have the right plan.
Pepys wrote all about me in his diary.
It was four days until I stopped,
I didn't want to go.
It was sad to go.
But I was all gone.
All my red family and friends went.
What am I?

Answer: *The Great Fire of London.*

Sofia Hoque (7)
Cranbrook Primary School, Ilford

What Am I?

I am an event in history.
I was like a giant mouth wide open.
I started in a bakery and I blazed and blazed.
I was the biggest one of all.
I was a big threat to everyone.
I produced thick black smoke.
How dangerous, threatening, hungry, difficult to defeat and bad I was!
I was a huge nightmare
Also I killed six to eight people.
One of the baker's maids was the first person I killed.
I happened in 1666, in Thomas Farriner's bakery in Pudding Lane.
What am I?

Answer: *The Great Fire of London.*

Luke Lyons-Adamson (6)
Cranbrook Primary School, Ilford

Night Destroyer

In the night, I scared people when it was hot.
In winter I usually hid from snow and Ice.
I was hot and I passed on from house to house.
People were scared of me, but I was scared of water.
People were rude to me all the time I appeared.
People broke my heart and destroyed me until I died.
I easily passed from one thing to another.
People hated me and my red friends a lot.
I woke up lots of people in London.
What am I?

Answer: *The Great Fire of London*.

Jan Denderski (7)
Cranbrook Primary School, Ilford

The Red Destroyer

I burnt down St Paul's Cathedral.
The whole of London woke because of me.
When I go near wood be worried!
When the wind changed direction, I got bigger.
I am as hot as lava!
I spread from house to house.
The people were scared of me, but I was afraid of water.
A person wrote all about me.
I started on the second of September 1666.
I ended at the end of a road.
I was really fierce.
What am I?

Answer: The Great Fire of London.

Uzayr Hussain (7)
Cranbrook Primary School, Ilford

What Is It?

Shockingly, it was a big, enormous nightmare for everyone in the town.
Luckily only a few people died.
It sucked up everything in the city like a vacuum cleaner.
What a sad day in history it was.
It was like a furious monster.
Surprisingly, it started in a bakery.
It was in 1666.
The Duke commanded to use gunpowder to destroy all of the houses.
What is it?

Answer: The Great Fire of London.

Alexandra Miron (6)
Cranbrook Primary School, Ilford

What Is It?

It lit the dark.
It was like a monster!
It was scary!
It was fierce and famous.
It ate houses, churches and schools.
Lots of people died.
Lots of it was spreading.
You could see it for miles and miles.
It was really tall, as tall as a cloud!
It blazed and blazed for three days!
It started at Pudding Lane.
What is it?

Answer: *The Great Fire of London.*

Hadiya Izzat (6)
Cranbrook Primary School, Ilford

What Is It?

It leapt like a monster.
It gobbled everything up that was in its way, even every tiny piece of wood.
It was so strong and fast that it gobbled a whole city.
They tried to put it out, but it was too strong.
It spread so quickly.
Buckets of water weren't enough to put it out.
It leapt so high that it could touch the sky.
What is it?

Answer: *The Great Fire of London.*

Aleeza Z Qadir (6)
Cranbrook Primary School, Ilford

What Is It?

It was a horrible beast that gobbled up the town.
It was a bad blazing night.
On Tuesday, St Paul's Cathedral was destroyed.
It was a nightmare they were all dreading.
People had to rebuild their houses.
It started in a bakery, by accident, on Pudding Lane.
It lasted from the second to the sixth September 1666.
What is it?

Answer: *The Great Fire of London.*

Milan Mistry (7)
Cranbrook Primary School, Ilford

The Red Destroyer

I am strong and long.
I lit in the dark like a tiny spark.
I started in an oven.
I started in a bakery.
I will scare you away, so run.
I am hot and dangerous.
They put me out with gunpowder.
If you touch me, your finger will burn.
I lasted for four days.
People threw buckets of water to stop me spreading.
What am I?

Answer: *The Great Fire of London.*

Ayman Patel (7)
Cranbrook Primary School, Ilford

What Am I?

I was like a dragon that swallowed houses.
Thousands of homes were destroyed.
I burnt for three days and three nights.
I was a nightmare they'd all been dreading.
What a dreadful night it was.
The Duke yelled, "Quick."
The baker woke to thick, black smoke.
He had never seen such a thing!
What am I?

Answer: *The Great Fire of London.*

Sulaiman Patel (7)
Cranbrook Primary School, Ilford

What Is It?

It was a horrible monster.
It gobbled up shops and houses.
Shockingly, it started on Pudding Lane in a baker's shop.
At one in the morning, lots of people died.
Some people survived.
It was hard to put out.
It was a dreadful nightmare for the people of London.
It was a very sad event in history.
What is it?

Answer: *The Great Fire of London.*

Shahmeer Khan (7)
Cranbrook Primary School, Ilford

What Is It?

It blazed and blazed.
It was a nightmare they'd been dreading!
It was like a monster creeping to wooden houses, churches and schools.
It started many, many years ago.
It was an event of history.
What a horrible day they had.
It swallowed wooden buildings for a long time.
What is it?

Answer: *The Great Fire of London.*

Mya Kaur (6)
Cranbrook Primary School, Ilford

What Is It?

It gobbled lots of homes.
What a bad day in history it was.
It woke everyone up because they made the bells ring.
It was very hard to get out.
It was a big fiery monster.
It could suck you up!
It threatened everyone.
It destroyed the biggest city in the world!
What is it?

Answer: *The Great Fire of London.*

Ahmed Ali Ibrahim (7)
Cranbrook Primary School, Ilford

What Is It?

It looked like a dinosaur eating all the houses.
The dinosaur ate all the bakery.
It blazed and blazed for three days and three nights.
The baker was sad because of the hot fire.
Everyone ran to the boats to try and get away.
It was a nightmare for all the people.
What is it?

Answer: The Great Fire of London.

Anaiyah Shafiq-Robinson (7)
Cranbrook Primary School, Ilford

What Am I?

I have very prickly spikes on my back.
I have pointy ears so I can protect myself from danger.
I have a long snout for shuffling in the pitch-dark night.
I curl up into a ball to protect my mummy.
I eat frogs, rats, bird's eggs and lizards.
What am I?

Answer: A hedgehog.

Michael Austin Culloty (6)
Darlinghurst Academy, Leigh-On-Sea

What Am I?

I have long, webbed wings.
I look black and grey.
I eat juicy fruit and some of us suck blood.
I live in a dark, gloomy cave.
I silently swoop through the night.
I use echolocation to hunt for food.
My body has got fur all over.
What am I?

Answer: A bat.

Elsie Newson (6)
Darlinghurst Academy, Leigh-On-Sea

What Am I?

I have tiny black eyes.
I hibernate during the winter.
I live in a warm cosy place.
I eat worms and slugs.
I am a gardener's friend.
I will curl up into a ball to protect myself from predators.
What am I?

Answer: A hedgehog.

Henry Dylan Giles (5)
Darlinghurst Academy, Leigh-On-Sea

What Am I?

I have short legs.
I hibernate in winter.
Then I wake up in the spring.
I come out at night to catch food.
I have spines to keep myself safe from predators.
I eat worms and slugs.
What am I?

Answer: A hedgehog.

Jeffrey Tinnams (5)
Darlinghurst Academy, Leigh-On-Sea

What Am I?

I have very pointy, sharp spines.
I live in warm, cosy places.
I like to eat slimy, juicy slugs.
I hibernate during the winter.
I curl up into a ball when I am scared.
What am I?

Answer: A hedgehog.

Evie Grace Coubrough (5)
Darlinghurst Academy, Leigh-On-Sea

Who Am I?

I live in the pitch-black night.
I have spines on my back to keep me out of danger.
I do not have prickly spines on my tummy.
I sniff underground.
I eat my prey.
What am I?

Answer: A hedgehog.

Freya Cardew (6)
Darlinghurst Academy, Leigh-On-Sea

What Am I?

I hibernate in the winter.
I wake up in spring.
I sleep on a nest of leaves.
I like to eat worms, snails and slugs.
I am a gardener's friend.
What am I?

Answer: A hedgehog.

Nathaniel Seabrook (5)
Darlinghurst Academy, Leigh-On-Sea

What Am I?

I have a long snout for shuffling underground.
I look through nests to find some yummy eggs.
I have sharp, pointy spines to keep me safe.
What am I?

Answer: A hedgehog.

Nancy Inmonger (6)
Darlinghurst Academy, Leigh-On-Sea

What Am I?

I am nocturnal.
I am orange and white.
I hunt my prey at night.
I have a bushy tail.
I eat animals that are smaller than myself.
What am I?

Answer: A fox.

Miriam Adesida (5)
Darlinghurst Academy, Leigh-On-Sea

What Am I?

I hunt in the pitch-black, spooky night.
I have a long, bushy tail.
I live underground in dens.
My favourite food is jam sandwiches.
What am I?

Answer: A fox.

Marilyn Roberts (6)
Darlinghurst Academy, Leigh-On-Sea

Spiky

I can roll.
I have five thousand spines.
I have tiny legs.
I have a tiny snout.
I can curl into a ball.
I eat worms.
What am I?

Answer: A hedgehog.

Devon Riley Carrier (6)
Darlinghurst Academy, Leigh-On-Sea

What Am I?

I have short legs.
I have thick fur.
I have sharp claws to dig.
I live in a big hole called a sett.
I have small eyes.
What am I?

Answer: A badger.

Mia Forbes (5)
Darlinghurst Academy, Leigh-On-Sea

Feathery

I have two brown wings.
I have a black beak.
I have sharp claws.
I have big wings.
I eat worms.
I can fly.
What am I?

Answer: An owl.

Callum Knight (5)
Darlinghurst Academy, Leigh-On-Sea

What Am I?

I have sharp spines.
I have black eyes.
I like to eat worms, slugs and snails.
I live in gardens and parks.
What am I?

Answer: A hedgehog.

Alistair Jopling (5)
Darlinghurst Academy, Leigh-On-Sea

Flappy

I have long wings.
I have sharp teeth.
I have long whiskers.
I eat fruit.
I have fur on my body.
What am I?

Answer: A bat.

Florence (6)
Darlinghurst Academy, Leigh-On-Sea

Small And Sweet

I grow in the spring.
I am sweet, juicy and small.
I change my colours like green, yellow and red.
I have many small spikes outside of my body.
Children like me very much.
Some people use me in cake and used me in jam.
What am I?

Answer: A strawberry.

Muhammad Azan (6)
Five Elms Primary School, Dagenham

Muffy

Cute and fluffy.
My name is Muffy.
I can run really quick.
I may give your face a lick.
I am cuddly and playful.
I will make your heart feel full.
I have four feet and mainly eat meat.
I have whiskers and a tail.
What am I?

Answer: A cat.

Jessica Boyd (6)
Five Elms Primary School, Dagenham

What Am I?

This animal is colourful
It's as fast as a truck.
It is white.
It might bite you and kick you.
It sits and can run.
It has a horn.
It is sparkly white with pink hair.
Sometimes it's purple.
What is it?

Answer: A unicorn.

Alara Tufansoy (5)
Five Elms Primary School, Dagenham

The Red Sweetness

I am red and juicy.
I am fresh with a taste of sweetness.
I can be served in a milkshake or ice cream
Children want me and adults need me.
I am the cutest of all the other fruits.
What am I?

Answer: A strawberry.

Sean Ampansah (6)
Five Elms Primary School, Dagenham

What Am I?

I like to run for miles and miles.
Sometimes I am small and sometimes I am big.
Sometimes a person likes to ride on me.
I come in different colours as you can see.
What am I?

Answer: A horse.

Francesca Michaels-Hayter (5)
Five Elms Primary School, Dagenham

What Am I?

I stand on one leg and my other one is behind.
I'm pink and I have a beak.
I have black eyes.
I can fly but I don't like it.
I can hop.
What am I?

Answer: A flamingo.

Osayantin Osunbor (6)
Five Elms Primary School, Dagenham

African Beast

I have a long tail.
I have a fluffy mane.
I have a mighty body.
I have four strong paws.
I have an orange body.
I am the king of the jungle.
What am I?

Answer: A lion.

Jeremy Yeboah (6)
Five Elms Primary School, Dagenham

Stripy Tiger

I like meat
But, I hate grass.
I hunt at night
So, don't come near.
I have sharp teeth,
I might bite.
I am a stripy big cat.
What am I?

Answer: A tiger.

Shanujah Jegatheesan (7)
Five Elms Primary School, Dagenham

Secret Creatures

Big round bowl,
Full of water,
With little stones
And seaweed inside.
Aquatic plants kept and displayed.
With small creatures inside.
What am I?

Answer: A fish.

Samanta Saldukaite (6)
Five Elms Primary School, Dagenham

Beautiful Wings

I popped out of the cocoon.
I started to fly.
I have beautiful colours on my little wings.
I love colourful flowers.
I am peaceful.
What am I?

Answer: A butterfly.

Lily-Belle Bryan (6)
Five Elms Primary School, Dagenham

What Am I?

I have orange fur.
I have black stripes.
I can roar.
I am very creepy.
I can sneak up to people.
I can just have a little bite.
What am I?

Answer: A tiger.

Esther Kyerewaa Tabi (5)
Five Elms Primary School, Dagenham

The Swinger

I am cheeky.
I like bananas.
I like swinging around.
I have two hands.
I have two feet.
I am brown.
I am in a zoo.
What am I?

Answer: A monkey.

Lily-May Oyewumi (5)
Five Elms Primary School, Dagenham

What Am I?

I have a long neck and I eat plants.
I live in mostly warm places.
I don't eat fish or bananas.
I have two eyes.
What am I?

Answer: A giraffe.

Mariam Musharaf (5)
Five Elms Primary School, Dagenham

Animal Spy

I spy, I spy,
I am spotty not dotty.
Fast not slow.
If my prey sees me they'll surely know.
I spy, I spy.
What am I?

Answer: A cheetah.

Paul Parkinson (7)
Five Elms Primary School, Dagenham

The Animal

I peek but I also sneak.
I have black stripes.
I have orange skin.
I have sharp claws.
I also have sharp teeth.
What am I?

Answer: A tiger.

Aqeeb Ali (6)
Five Elms Primary School, Dagenham

Cute Pets

I have whiskers.
I chase mice.
I have a tail.
I run fast.
I have yellow eyes.
I'm a pet.
Can you guess what am I?

Answer: A cat.

Macie Twiggs (6)
Five Elms Primary School, Dagenham

The Disgusting Animal

I'm very silly.
I am ugly.
I have eyes on my head.
I have many eyes.
I'm slimy.
I look shiny.
What am I?

Answer: An alien.

Moyin Emmanuella Akintunde (7)
Five Elms Primary School, Dagenham

Adorable

They are cute.
They don't mute.
They are not tall, but small.
They are cuddly.
Not ugly.
What are they?

Answer: Babies.

Annabel Chiamaka Omereonye (6)
Five Elms Primary School, Dagenham

What Am I?

I have a long neck.
I like to eat plants.
I live in warm places.
I like water.
I am very tall
What am I?

Answer: A giraffe.

Alessia Maria Ciorba (6)
Five Elms Primary School, Dagenham

The Sneaky One

I like to eat people and sneak up on people.
I am long.
But I do not have legs.
I am slithery.
What am I?

Answer: A snake.

Bailey Brodie (6)
Five Elms Primary School, Dagenham

What Am I?

Sometimes I am big or small.
I have black spots and yellow skin.
I have four legs.
What am I?

Answer: A cheetah.

Alfie Martin (5)
Five Elms Primary School, Dagenham

Icy Weather

I keep you warm, never make you cold.
I can belong to anyone, small or old.
You can find me in any colour and in any size.
You may want to use me at sunrise.
I am not seen all the time, only when it's not hot outside.
I do not need food and drink to survive
As I am not alive.
However, I can be fluffy and so cuddly.
I am needed to warm your cold, chilly hands.
What am I?

Answer: A pair of gloves.

Shakirah Haque (6)
Furze Infant School, Chadwell Heath

Venomous Power

I swallow my food
When I'm in a bad mood.

I shed my skin
But it doesn't go into a bin.

I lay eggs
But I don't have any legs.

Mostly I live in Asia or Africa
But I also can be found in Australia.

I have fangs
But I don't have any bangs.

I am a reptile
And my venom is vile.

What am I?

Answer: A snake.

James Hernon (6)
Furze Infant School, Chadwell Heath

Luscious Leaves

I have branches of leaves on the dusty floor.
I am super colourful.
The wind whistles in the dusty trees.
Every day is the same, a dark and gloomy morning.
A great time for adventures discovering the leaves.
But something that is beautiful,
Is the birds chirping way
Brightening up the day.
What am I?

Answer: Autumn.

Hamas Kakar (7)
Furze Infant School, Chadwell Heath

The Pretty Thing

I am unique.
I have so many pets.
I can play the flute.
I am rich.
So many boys love me.
I sing to birds.
I have servants.
I have lots of jewels.
I go to lots of parties.
I have beautiful hair.
I wear puffy dresses.
I rule the land.
What am I?

Answer: A princess.

Ademide Elizabeth Ogunmokun (6)
Furze Infant School, Chadwell Heath

It's About Time!

I have hands but no body.
I have a face but no eyes to see.
I can't see you when you look at me.
I can be found in almost every room.
I can let you know when to watch cartoons.
I can be big and I can be small.
I am usually found on the wall.
What am I?

Answer: A clock.

Sulaiman Qadir (7)
Furze Infant School, Chadwell Heath

Fast Flyer

I'm small, but quite chubby.
I know how to tweet.
I'm quite rare.
You normally see me in winter or spring.
I have a beak and tiny feet.
I have wings.
I'm brown and red on my tummy.
My name is the name of Batman's sidekick.
What am I?

Answer: A robin.

Michaela Atulomah (7)
Furze Infant School, Chadwell Heath

Electricity On Road

I have four tyres, all on wheels.
To build me, you need lots of steel.
I can have four or more seats
And from the radio you can hear music.
Sometimes you need diesel or petrol.
I mainly use electricity.
I drive around the city.
What am I?

Answer: Electric car.

Jakub Powaga (7)
Furze Infant School, Chadwell Heath

Style

It takes only a short while.
I can give you a nice style.
Don't go away, just stop.
I have for you, a lollipop
Either come with Dad or Mum.
You will see me with scissors and a comb.
Some children laugh and some cry.
What am I?

Answer: A hairdresser.

Eshaal Fatima Zaidi (6)
Furze Infant School, Chadwell Heath

Round And Round

I am round like a ball, but I don't roll.
I can be in the dark and in the light.
People live on me near the sea.
I have creatures big and small.
You can see me from space looking blue and green.
I'm made of land and sea.
What am I?

Answer: The Earth.

Ishaq Amin (6)
Furze Infant School, Chadwell Heath

My Favourite Treat

I'm cold and nice.
Good for a treat.
I come in different flavours.
I am made of milk.
I can have toppings, like sprinkles or a flake.
I am crunchy on the bottom.
On the top I am nice sweet and just like cream.
What am I?

Answer: Ice cream.

Isabel Ruby Arunachalam (7)
Furze Infant School, Chadwell Heath

Power

I am the fastest land animal in the world.
I am stylish with furry black spots.
I have got a yellowish, tan body.
Beware!
I have got semi-retractable claws!
Hunting is my major duty.
I walk around Asia and Africa.
What am I?

Answer: A cheetah.

Tameem Wahhaj (6)
Furze Infant School, Chadwell Heath

A Sugary Surprise

I grow in tropical countries.
I can grow up to six metres long.
You can find me in a fruit market.
You can peel my green stalk.
You can eat my yellowy-white inside.
I am very sweet.
You can make sweets out of me.
What am I?

Answer: *Sugar cane.*

Maeasha Noor (6)
Furze Infant School, Chadwell Heath

Vehicle Power

I have four wheels.
I am smaller than a double-decker bus.
I'm the most popular vehicle in the world.
I start with a 'C' and end with a 'R'.
Sometimes, I live in a garage.
Sometimes, I live on the road.
What am I?

Answer: A car.

Saad Amin Mitru (7)
Furze Infant School, Chadwell Heath

A Burner

I'm long when I'm young.
I'm short when I am old.
I am quite handy when there is no light.
I can smell sweet.
I have a flame.
I am a gift that will last long.
I can smell beautiful in your home.
What am I?

Answer: A Yankee Candle.

Akashdeep Rylee Singh (6)
Furze Infant School, Chadwell Heath

Locomotion

You can use me to get around,
Through the city, country or town.
Heavy load I sometimes carry.
I use steam, diesel or electricity.
The journey may be very long,
And sometimes even underground.

What am I?

Answer: A train.

Jonathan Pinard (6)
Furze Infant School, Chadwell Heath

Bouncy Fun

I am round and bouncy.
I come in different sizes, small, medium or large.
I can make you bounce high up in the air.
Children feel happy and excited when they see me.
I stay outside in the garden.
What am I?

Answer: A trampoline.

Raiha Pabani (6)
Furze Infant School, Chadwell Heath

Fluffy

You can find me in North America.
Females of me are called does.
I live in groups.
I like to hop and take loops.
I live for about ten years.
And let's not forget I have very long ears.
What am I?

Answer: A rabbit.

Amina Begum (7)
Furze Infant School, Chadwell Heath

What Am I?

I am strong and stripy, fast and fierce.
I might be orange.
I am a meat-eater.
I have very sharp teeth.
I live in a jungle.
I live in Asia.
I like to move around the jungle.
What am I?

Answer: A tiger.

Ali Adeel (7)
Furze Infant School, Chadwell Heath

Not The Sky, But The Sea

I am alive.
I live in the sea.
I can't swim or dive.
I don't have eyes, so I can't see light.
I always stick to things.
I look like something in the sky at night.
What am I?

Answer: A starfish.

Issa Renato Morgante (6)
Furze Infant School, Chadwell Heath

Great Giant

I am the strongest in the world.
I weigh up to five tonnes (5000kg)
You can find two types of me.
I roll around in mud.
I am grey.
I am the largest land animal in the world.
What am I?

Answer: An elephant.

Alan Idriss Abiji (6)
Furze Infant School, Chadwell Heath

Ultimate Speed

I am the fastest land runner.
I have two black stripes on my face.
I make different sounds.
I like to sit on the rock.
I use my tail to guide me.
I can see my prey far away.
What am I?

Answer: A cheetah.

Leke Toluwanimi Aiyemo-Abiwo (7)
Furze Infant School, Chadwell Heath

Sticky Feet

I have big eyes.
My tongue is very long.
My favourite food is flies.
I can stick on a tree.
I mostly walk near branches to see if there are any flies.
I can camouflage.
What am I?

Answer: A chameleon.

Amy Yaa Abiji (6)
Furze Infant School, Chadwell Heath

Insect

I could live in trees
I eat little pieces of food.
You could find me outside houses.
I have antennae.
I can be a kid or an adult.
I am really black.
I have four legs.
What am I?

Answer: An ant.

Anthony Deaconeasa (6)
Furze Infant School, Chadwell Heath

Scary Sea Monster

I come in all shapes and sizes.
I eat fish.
I have big eyes.
I have sharp teeth.
I swim fast.
I have two fins.
People are scared of me.
I am an amazing animal.
What am I?

Answer: A shark.

Schalk Steyn (7)
Furze Infant School, Chadwell Heath

Animal

I live on a tree.
I make sticky webs.
I have eight legs.
I am black.
People are scared of me.
I hide anywhere.
I live on my web.
I can walk up and down walls.
What am I?

Answer: A spider.

Joshua Samuels (7)
Furze Infant School, Chadwell Heath

Box On The Wall

I have a very slim or chunky body.
People sit around me all the time.
I entertain, educate or disappoint.
I always look good in colour.
The young and the old love me.
What am I?

Answer: A television.

Monique Isaac (6)
Furze Infant School, Chadwell Heath

Bearded Dragon

I am a small animal.
I have a long tail and four legs.
I am mainly green, brown, blue or yellow.
I run very fast.
I live in warm places.
I like to eat sweet fruit.
What am I?

Answer: A lizard.

Sara Hussain (6)
Furze Infant School, Chadwell Heath

Slippery Sue

I am sometimes blue.
I am pretty.
I love cold weather.
I am dripping wet.
I melt in the heat.
I love being in the freezer.
I'm as white as the clouds.
What am I?

Answer: A snowflake.

Lale Kussan (6)
Furze Infant School, Chadwell Heath

What Am I?

I am very fast and swift.
Eating meat is my favourite meal.
I hunt and hide.
Enemies can't catch me.
I am spotty, not stripy.
If you see me, you will run.
What am I?

Answer: A cheetah.

Milan Vyas (7)
Furze Infant School, Chadwell Heath

Travel In The Sky

It is a huge egg shell,
But it may have different sizes.
Metal is in its veins.
It has its own nest.
It goes everywhere.
People enjoy sitting on there.
What is it?

Answer: An aeroplane.

Tanjimul Haque (6)
Furze Infant School, Chadwell Heath

Madagascar

I have stripes.
I run fast from side to side.
I stand up while sleeping.
I have excellent eyesight and hearing.
I have two colours.
A crossing has my name.
What am I?

Answer: A zebra.

Nyah White-Laud (7)
Furze Infant School, Chadwell Heath

What Am I?

I don't have a mouth, so I can't talk.
I do have legs but I can't walk.
I'm not a bag nor a sack.
But I have a back.
Without me a table is bare.
What am I?

Answer: A chair.

Tanisha Qyra Noim (7)
Furze Infant School, Chadwell Heath

Arctic

I am white and fluffy.
I have black beady eyes.
My nose is shiny.
I live in the cold.
I am surrounded by snow.
I can camouflage with my habitat.
What am I?

Answer: An Arctic fox.

Khadijah Jannath (6)
Furze Infant School, Chadwell Heath

What Am I?

I am cold.
I am light.
I am coming from the sky.
Children love me a lot.
And I cover all your house.
If you touch me a lot, I can make you cold and wet.
What am I?

Answer: Snow.

Domas Dackevicius (6)
Furze Infant School, Chadwell Heath

Catch Me If You Can

I am the fastest in the wild
I can run up to 120km/h.
I hunt for my food.
I have short fur.
I am one colour with spots.
I am a meat-eater.
What am I?

Answer: A cheetah.

Tyler Zachary Frederick (6)
Furze Infant School, Chadwell Heath

Noisy And Fast

I make a noise.
I have four wheels.
You can hear me from faraway.
I have a hose and a ladder.
I like red colour.
Always ready to help.
What am I?

Answer: A fire truck.

Robert Iuzcov (6)
Furze Infant School, Chadwell Heath

Royal

I can be seen in movies.
I can have long or short hair.
I sit on a throne.
I wear a tiara.
I am a royal.
I am the daughter of a queen.
What am I?

Answer: A princess.

Aroush Ashraf Ahasan (6)
Furze Infant School, Chadwell Heath

What Am I?

I roam the African wild,
I hunt for my prey.
Sometimes I will do a fierce roar,
I have a furry mane.
All the time I am the king of the jungle.
What am I?

Answer: A lion.

Zaina Mahmood (7)
Furze Infant School, Chadwell Heath

Long Neck

I don't get eaten.
I don't hunt.
I eat leaves.
I live in Africa.
I can see high but not low.
I have a long neck.
What am I?

Answer: A giraffe.

Eva Mana (7)
Furze Infant School, Chadwell Heath

What Am I?

I have sharp teeth.
I live in the jungle.
I am king of the jungle.
I have no claws.
I eat meat.
I have a mane.
What am I?

Answer: A lion.

Tanzeela Hussain (6)
Furze Infant School, Chadwell Heath

Summer Day

I would only come out in the day.
I am bright and shimmery.
I make light.
I make people happy.
I make things grow.
What am I?

Answer: *The sun.*

Erin Young (6)
Furze Infant School, Chadwell Heath

Tall

I have short hair.
I have skin
And I have patterns.
I have four legs.
I have bones.
I have four stomachs.
What am I?

Answer: A giraffe.

Aiden Chipungu (6)
Furze Infant School, Chadwell Heath

What Am I?

I have sharp teeth
I am very fast.
I have four legs.
I have long whiskers
I am very bright.
I am furry.
What am I?

Answer: A tiger.

Jasmine Begum (6)
Furze Infant School, Chadwell Heath

What Am I?

I can be any colour.
I can go far away.
I can go fast.
I come in any size.
What am I?

Answer: A car.

Jayden Richards (7)
Furze Infant School, Chadwell Heath

The Copycat

I have colourful feathers.
I can squawk very loud.
I am a medium-sized.
My house is very high.
Sometimes I live in a pet shop.
I don't like naughty animals.
I always fly high in the blue sky.
Sometimes I live in high trees.
When I fly high, I can see other animals.
What am I?

Answer: A parrot.

Joshua Spry (5)
Gidea Park Primary School, Gidea Park

Fast Runner

I am white, black and brown.
I have patches and I have sharp teeth.
I can run really fast like a cheetah.
I have a curved tail like a pig.
I like to eat meat from my owner.
I do not like really loud noises.
When I see a cat I chase it.
I bury bones underground.
What am I?

Answer: A dog.

Oliver Ian Swider (5)
Gidea Park Primary School, Gidea Park

Fast Trot

I live in a field.
I can trot fast.
I have brown skin.
I don't pounce.
I have a white tail.
I like eating grass.
I have pointy ears.
I swish my tail.
I like to trot with my friends.
I would be happy with my friends.
What am I?

Answer: A horse.

Violet Bulmer (5)
Gidea Park Primary School, Gidea Park

Cute Babies

I have white and black stripes.
I can climb on trees.
I am bigger than my baby.
My baby is cute and cuddly.
Sometimes I am friendly.
I growl.
I like bamboo.
I don't like humans.
I get angry when I get hyper.
What am I?

Answer: A panda bear.

Inaya Ahmed (5)
Gidea Park Primary School, Gidea Park

The Quiet Hunter

I have a soft tail.
I can run very fast.
I can jump very high.
You can't have me for a pet.
I have green eyes.
I have brown fur.
I like to eat little creatures.
I have a white bobble.
I have some pink in my ears.
What am I?

Answer: A fox.

Olivia Killick (6)
Gidea Park Primary School, Gidea Park

Silent Runner

If you touch me I might bite.
I have sharp teeth.
I like hunting for food.
I might be in a zoo.
The end of my tail is white.
I live in the forest.
You might hunt for me.
I eat meat.
I have big ears so I can hear you.
What am I?

Answer: A fox.

Portia Holton (6)
Gidea Park Primary School, Gidea Park

The Flying Insect

I am yellow and black.
I fly in the air and look for honey in colourful ones.
I live in a yellow hive which is very sticky.
I have transparent wings.
Sometimes I sting people when they are mean to me.
I live in a garden or a zoo.
What am I?

Answer: A bee.

Lexi Zhao (5)
Gidea Park Primary School, Gidea Park

Good Climber

I have black and white stripes.
I am a good climber.
When my cubs are born, they are pink and cute.
They don't have fur when they are babies.
I lick my cubs to protect them.
I like to eat bamboo when I'm hungry.
What am I?

Answer: A panda.

Nicole Racila (5)
Gidea Park Primary School, Gidea Park

The Rainbow Wings

Sometimes I sit on a flower and I fly as well.
I have rainbow wings.
Sometimes I am patterned as well.
I always fly and flutter.
I have transparent, soft, sparkly wings.
I am colourful.
I have symmetrical wings.
What am I?

Answer: A butterfly.

Niharika Sharma (6)
Gidea Park Primary School, Gidea Park

Good Protector

I have the cutest baby in the world.
I can protect myself from other animals.
I have dry skin because of the hot sun.
I like water, so I can cool down.
I live in a very hot country or a zoo.
I love my baby.
What am I?

Answer: A rhinoceros.

Lennaea McGowan (6)
Gidea Park Primary School, Gidea Park

Silent Flutter

I like to flutter into the trees.
I have no fur.
I ate my egg when I was born.
I was born as a caterpillar.
When I grow up I will taste with my feet.
I have delicate wings that flutter in the wind.
What am I?

Answer: A butterfly.

Ria Patel (6)
Gidea Park Primary School, Gidea Park

The Copycat

I have a black, sharp, speckled beak.
Sometimes I live in the zoo unless I live in the jungle.
I live in tropical places.
I have rainbow feathers.
I can live in a pet shop.
I can copy other people.
What am I?

Answer: A parrot.

Alice Evelyn Corkin (5)
Gidea Park Primary School, Gidea Park

The Furry Hunter

I can jump high.
I can jump on places.
I have sharp teeth.
I have yellow fur with black spots.
I can run.
I can hiss.
I can hide.
I have pointy teeth.
I have long whiskers.
What am I?

Answer: A cat.

George Moore (5)
Gidea Park Primary School, Gidea Park

Flying Animal

I have white fur.
I have wings.
I live in the forest.
My wings are made out of feathers.
I gallop.
I skip.
I look like a horse when I am a baby.
I run fast.
I am kind.
What am I?

Answer: A unicorn.

Eirene Kalliopi Palamaras (5)
Gidea Park Primary School, Gidea Park

Spiky Friend

I have a spiky back.
I am brown.
I can roll myself into a ball.
I eat worms by digging in the dirt.
I have a fluffy belly.
I always roll down the hill.
I come out at night.
What am I?

Answer: A hedgehog.

Lola Prescott (6)
Gidea Park Primary School, Gidea Park

Dangerous Animal

I have sharp claws.
I live in the zoo.
I scratch other animals.
I like to sleep in the sun.
I have ropes to climb on.
I have orange and black striped fur.
I am a meat-eater.
What am I?

Answer: A tiger.

Henry Wakeling (6)
Gidea Park Primary School, Gidea Park

The Rainbow Fire

I live in the field.
My body is white.
I have a stripy horn.
My hair is soft.
I can gallop fast.
I have wings.
My tail is long.
My tail is soft.
I am magic.
What am I?

Answer: A unicorn.

Francesca Davie (6)
Gidea Park Primary School, Gidea Park

The Colour Changer

I have rough green skin.
I can use camouflage when scared.
Animals hunt for me.
I live in a pet shop.
I can run really fast.
No one can see me.
I am medium-sized.
What am I?

Answer: A chameleon.

Alexander Aye (6)
Gidea Park Primary School, Gidea Park

The Colourful Creature

I can fly up in the sky.
I make brown things.
I eat silky plants.
I have colourful silky wings.
I can turn into another creature.
I only come out in the summer.
What am I?

Answer: A butterfly.

Millie Grimes (6)
Gidea Park Primary School, Gidea Park

The Squawker

I live in a tropical place.
I am a tropical animal.
My home is a zoo.
Sometimes I sit on a branch.
I always fly through the blue sky.
I like eating crunchy seeds.
What am I?

Answer: A parrot.

Harrison Sutton-Evans (5)
Gidea Park Primary School, Gidea Park

The Black And Brown Creature

I have a spiky back.
I can crawl.
I am soft on my bottom.
I am black and brown.
I am smaller than a dog.
I have little legs.
I can curl up in a ball.
What am I?

Answer: A hedgehog.

Zachary Tran (5)
Gidea Park Primary School, Gidea Park

The Creature

I live on the grass.
I gallop around.
I have a mane.
I run fast.
A princess rides me.
I have four legs.
I have blue eyes.
I have colourful hair.
What am I?

Answer: A unicorn.

Chloe Marcou (6)
Gidea Park Primary School, Gidea Park

The Good Climber

If you come close to me.
I might hurt you.
I am black and white.
I am a dangerous creature.
I have a furry body.
I have big ears.
I have a curly tail.
What am I?

Answer: A panda.

Tia Blenman (6)
Gidea Park Primary School, Gidea Park

The Good Climber

I have a furry body.
My favourite thing to eat is bamboo.
I can climb tall trees.
I have dangerous claws.
I have black and white fur.
I have cute babies.
What am I?

Answer: A panda.

Jessica Mawer (6)
Gidea Park Primary School, Gidea Park

The Woof

I live in a sparkly house.
I have blue fiery eyes.
I have chew sticks and bones.
I have white and brown fur.
I can run fast outside.
I play with my owner.
What am I?

Answer: A dog.

Samuel David Weatherly (6)
Gidea Park Primary School, Gidea Park

The Tropical Copycat

I have a black beak.
I have rainbow feathers.
Sometimes I can live in the pet shop.
I can repeat other people.
I can jump fast in a tree.
I am soft.
What am I?

Answer: A parrot.

Kendra Akua Lord (6)
Gidea Park Primary School, Gidea Park

What Am I?

I have orangey brown fur.
I can live in a tree in the zoo or the jungle.
I can squeeze you.
I love swinging in the vines.
I like playing silly games.
What am I?

Answer: An orangutan.

Ethan George Bird (6)
Gidea Park Primary School, Gidea Park

The Tall Tree House

I have a long neck and long legs.
Sometimes when I am hungry I munch leaves.
I am the tallest animal in the world.
I can poke my head in a jeep safari truck.
What am I?

Answer: A giraffe.

Kiyarah Thomas (5)
Gidea Park Primary School, Gidea Park

Winged Creature

I have wings.
I can fly.
I have eyes.
I can be on a tree.
I have two legs.
I can eat insects.
I can hang upside down.
I live in a dark cave.
What am I?

Answer: A bat.

Lucie Hawkins (5)
Gidea Park Primary School, Gidea Park

The Milk Drinker

I have yellow, soft fur.
I can drink milk.
My home is the pet shop.
I like to be stroked.
I don't like scary things.
I sometimes like silly faces.
What am I?

Answer: A cat.

Melanie Deleu (6)
Gidea Park Primary School, Gidea Park

A Good Hopper

Sometimes you can see me in the park.
I like to go in holes.
I eat lettuce.
I can be a pet.
My eyes are like cocoa beans.
I like to flap my ears.
What am I?

Answer: A rabbit.

Rosie Winser-Shead (5)
Gidea Park Primary School, Gidea Park

Dangerous Jungle

I am yellow.
I have sharp teeth.
I have sharp claws.
I am a good hunter.
I have four legs.
I am a dangerous animal.
I am a furry animal.
What am I?

Answer: A lion.

Evan Rejek (5)
Gidea Park Primary School, Gidea Park

The Copycat

I have a black, sharp beak.
I live in the zoo.
I have colourful feathers.
I have green eyes.
I have a rainbow tail.
I squawk around.
What am I?

Answer: A parrot.

Tayte Ashcroft (5)
Gidea Park Primary School, Gidea Park

The Furball

I have brown and white fur.
I have floppy ears.
I can jump high.
I can run outside.
I am sometimes cute.
But sometimes, naughty.
What am I?

Answer: A dog.

Vanaya Joshi (5)
Gidea Park Primary School, Gidea Park

Friendly Animal

I can run outside.
I live at home.
I have brown fur.
I have a wet nose.
I have a big bone.
I like going for a long walk.
What am I?

Answer: A dog.

Kaiden Chambers (5)
Gidea Park Primary School, Gidea Park

The Best Flyer

I have red, hard skin.
My horn is white and sharp.
I can breathe fire.
I can fly high.
I have red wings.
I am scary.
What am I?

Answer: A dragon.

Tausif Ornob Islam (5)
Gidea Park Primary School, Gidea Park

The Bite

I have soft black fur.
I have sharp claws.
I live in a house.
I am small.
I am little and short.
I am a milk drinker.
What am I?

Answer: A cat.

Fraser Sowerby (6)
Gidea Park Primary School, Gidea Park

Fast Runner

I can climb trees.
I can hide nuts in big holes.
I can run fast.
I have a long tail.
When I see people I run away.
What am I?

Answer: A squirrel.

Toby Morton Woodman (6)
Gidea Park Primary School, Gidea Park

The High Flyer

I can eat carrots.
I can fly.
I have a red nose.
I fly at night and pull a sleigh.
I have horns.
What am I?

Answer: Rudolph the reindeer.

Hamish Jhurry (6)
Gidea Park Primary School, Gidea Park

The Climber

I can slither in a log.
I have teeth so I can bite you.
I can live in a pet shop.
I can roll over near the trees.
What am I?

Answer: A snake.

William Walker (5)
Gidea Park Primary School, Gidea Park

The Flyer With A Horn

I live in a lovely place.
I have a pink mane.
I am pink.
I was in a story.
I live with other animals.
What am I?

Answer: A unicorn.

Teja Zeimantaite (6)
Gidea Park Primary School, Gidea Park

Fluffy

I have sharp claws.
I like to lick my paws.
I have long whiskers.
I can run fast.
I like sleeping too.
What am I?

Answer: A cat.

Jack Sullivan (5)
Gidea Park Primary School, Gidea Park

Dangerous Animal

I black and round stripes.
I eat bamboo.
I can climb trees very well.
I am a very dangerous animal.
What am I?

Answer: A panda bear.

Connor Craydon (6)
Gidea Park Primary School, Gidea Park

Silent Creature

I live in the jungle.
I have orange and black fur.
I can jump in the jungle.
I have sharp claws.
What am I?

Answer: A tiger.

Dhruv Mistry (6)
Gidea Park Primary School, Gidea Park

Big Blue

I live in the sea.
I'm big and blue.
I swim in the ocean.
I am long.
I eat krill.
What am I?

Answer: A blue whale.

Jay Cheung (5)
Gidea Park Primary School, Gidea Park

What Am I?

I have eyes like a shark.
I can run fast with my legs.
I have shiny teeth.
I am really scary.
What am I?

Answer: A lion.

Thuy-Trang Nguyen (5)
Gidea Park Primary School, Gidea Park

The Fast Hunter

I have black spots.
I live in the jungle.
I eat other animals.
I leap on my prey.
What am I?

Answer: A leopard.

Hafi Kalota (6)
Gidea Park Primary School, Gidea Park

Wet Licker

I like to go to the park.
I have a pointy tail.
I have soft ears.
I have fluffy fur.
What am I?

Answer: A dog.

Rosie June Taylor (6)
Gidea Park Primary School, Gidea Park

Silent Hunter

I can jump high.
I have a soft tail.
I can leap.
I can run fast.
I am fluffy.
What am I?

Answer: A cat.

Shantel Agyei (5)
Gidea Park Primary School, Gidea Park

Big Head

I lay in the bushes.
I eat bugs.
I can stretch far.
I have a long body.
What am I?

Answer: A snake.

Marley Henry (5)
Gidea Park Primary School, Gidea Park

The Special Hunter

I have fur.
I have floppy ears.
I drink milk from a bowl.
I have a tail.
What am I?

Answer: A cat.

Mya Blenman (6)
Gidea Park Primary School, Gidea Park

Small Pet

I can run fast.
I eat bones.
I like sleeping.
I like to chase a stick.
What am I?

Answer: A puppy.

Riley Collins (5)
Gidea Park Primary School, Gidea Park

Climb On Trees

I have a furry tail.
I have two ears that are furry.
I live in a warm house.
What am I?

Answer: A cat.

Lois Lynch (6)
Gidea Park Primary School, Gidea Park

Noisy Pet

I can bark.
I can jump.
I am furry.
What am I?

Answer: A dog.

Lukas Lapuska (5)
Gidea Park Primary School, Gidea Park

Est.1991

YOUNG WRITERS INFORMATION

We hope you have enjoyed reading this book – and that you will continue to in the coming years.

If you're a young writer who enjoys reading and creative writing, or the parent of an enthusiastic poet or story writer, do visit our website **www.youngwriters.co.uk**. Here you will find free competitions, workshops and games, as well as recommended reads, a poetry glossary and our blog.

If you would like to order further copies of this book, or any of our other titles, then please give us a call or visit **www.youngwriters.co.uk**.

Young Writers
Remus House
Coltsfoot Drive
Peterborough
PE2 9BF
(01733) 890066
info@youngwriters.co.uk